100 PLUS DIVORCE TIPS™

Guide To Finding And Hiring A Winning Divorce Attorney

by Chris Dunnaville

100 Plus Tips™ LLC

**100 Plus Divorce Tips™ Guide To Finding And Hiring
A Winning Divorce Attorney**

Published by
100 Plus Tips™. LLC
P.O. Box 2306
Lake Oswego, OR 97035
WWW.100plustips.com

ISBN-13: 978-0692221457
ISBN-10: 069222145X

Contents

Dedication

To my beloved daughter Allie. I hope that you never need to use any of the tips in Dad's books

1. Introduction: Who Should Use This Book?

Are you thinking about getting a divorce? Perhaps you or your spouse has already made the decision, with one of you pulling the trigger to start the process. Now, do you find yourself smack in the middle of fighting for your life in a nasty divorce battle? No matter how long a couple has been together, most marriages that end as a result of divorce end contentiously. Trust becomes distrust, and love and romance are replaced by anger and hate.

This book is for people who want to take control of their divorce despite all of the anger, hate, and stress they may be feeling. The most important thing you can do to take control and *financially win* is to hire a great divorce attorney. In **100 Plus Divorce Tips™ Guide to Finding and Hiring a Winning Divorce Attorney**, you'll learn essential information on why and how to find an attorney who will make sure you get the best possible financial outcome from your divorce.

Find out:

- Why it is essential to assemble the right divorce team

- The seventeen characteristics of a winning divorce attorney

- What kind of law firm you need to win your specific divorce

- Why the gender of your divorce attorney matters

- How to find a winning divorce attorney: where to look and who to talk to

- Important questions to ask yourself and your attorney before you make a hire.

...And much more. If you know how to find the experienced divorce attorney who is right for you and your case, it *is* possible to turn your divorce into a victory.

2.
How to Win Your Divorce: Take Control by Getting the Right Help

For individuals going through the divorce process, life can feel like it has become burdened by a huge barrel of toxic waste. Typically, their days are filled with stress and sadness, which often leads to depression. I remember vividly how in my first divorce (I have been married and divorced twice), I could not sleep well at nights. It would be 2 or 3 AM in the morning and I would be lying in my bed tossing and turning. I thought about things like being alone, being a failure, and being unworthy of being loved. There were also worries about losing all of the assets that I had worked so hard to accumulate. The thoughts about what would become of my finances and the threat of financial loss were most troubling.

Many psychologists and sociologists put going through a divorce on par with experiencing the death of a close relative. How about you? Is this your current situation? Is this how you are feeling?

If this is your state of mind, the primary reason that you are feeling this way is probably that you are scared. You are scared about what is going to happen to you after the divorce and scared of all the possible changes that might occur in your life as a result of it.

In fact, if I could really get inside your head and pin you down, you might admit that the main thing that you are fearful of is the unknown. Specifically, you are afraid of not knowing what the final outcome of your divorce will be and how being divorced is going to affect the rest of your life. You are worried!

A large part of why you are worried might be that you have no idea how you will survive financially after the divorce. You may be thinking that the divorce will break you financially. As I mentioned, that is exactly what I was worried about. People going through divorce feel anxious because to a large extent, they feel powerless over controlling the final outcome. Not knowing what is going to happen to you and the fear of not surviving financially would be extremely stressful for most people.

I got to experience these feelings twice. I was especially stressed in my first divorce because the whole concept of divorce was new to me. I had no idea what to expect or how I would end up, other than knowing that the divorce would happen and that I wasn't going to be married anymore. By the time of my second divorce, I was a bit calmer. I knew from my first divorce experience that at the very least, I wasn't going to die.

Even though I knew that the world wasn't going to end, I was still anxious about my situation because I had a lot more at stake. I was older (in my forties) and I had a child, more assets, status in the community, responsibilities, etc. The good news is that with age often comes wisdom. During both divorces, I was smart enough to get professional support through a couple of different therapists. I got help to deal with all the stress. The therapists also helped me realize that for me and for most people, I was mainly stressed out and unable to sleep not so much because of the divorces themselves, but because I felt like I could not control the process or outcomes of my divorces.

What I realized was that for me to really feel at ease and sleep better at nights, I needed to feel a greater sense of control over my divorces, especially their financial aspects. The more I felt in control of my situation and the outcome of my divorces, the less stress I felt. The more in control I felt, the more powerful I felt. I would actually begin to get a bit of an adrenaline rush from having power over certain aspects of my divorces.

If this makes sense to you and if you can relate to what I am describing, take a deep breath and exhale a sigh of relief. I am going to help you to relax a bit and put most of your nervous feelings aside by giving you some solid advice. I will share tips on how you can greatly reduce your stress level by empowering yourself to be more in control of the outcome of your divorce. I am going to help you improve the odds of winning your divorce, both financially and emotionally. I want to help you win your divorce by not only getting what you want from it, but also understanding more about the divorce process, the financial side of getting divorced, and the things you need to look out for with regards to controlling the costs in your divorce. I will assist you by making sure that your final settlement or judgment is one that works in your favor in the long term. I want you to be happy as well as stable.

The tips that I give you will help you to gain a greater degree of control over your divorce and your finances. As a result of being more in control of your divorce, you will gain confidence about your divorce process, which will ease a lot of the stress and thus help to settle your emotions. The secrets to achieving this level of comfort are:

1. **Being properly prepared**

2. **Having the right resources available to you when you need them**

3. **Having a basic understanding of how the divorce process works here in the United States**

I am sure that by helping you with these three things, you will be able to sleep better at night and be better prepared to financially and emotionally win your divorce. I have learned a lot about divorce over the years, so much so that I have become an advisor on the subject, and I have helped a lot of people with planning and winning their divorces. A lot of my advice is information that you would not hear from attorneys because it is not within their expertise. Quite frankly, some of the information and ideas that I share would not be proper for an attorney to discuss with a client.

3. What Does it Mean to "Financially Win" Your Divorce?

Winning a divorce today is not an easy task, and there really aren't any outright guarantees. A couple of the key points that make winning a divorce difficult are that the people involved are generally pretty emotional and often irrational. Also, there are usually lots of people involved (including innocent children), and many of them have big egos. The egos can often get in the way of moving your case forward quickly. In addition, each state has its own way of doing things – you may get a result in one state that you wouldn't get in another state.

What does it mean to win a divorce financially? Anywhere in the US, this means dissolving your marriage with the least amount of financial and emotional pain possible. It also means obtaining your desired goals, which may include: getting custody of your children and securing maximum parenting time, maintaining ownership of specific assets such as a business, homes, automobiles, and pets, and paying the minimum or receiving the maximum amount of alimony available (depending on whether you are the payer or the payee).

There could be a whole host of other items (both tangible and intangible) that you might want to get out of your divorce in order to feel like you are the winner. Additionally, you will want to accomplish your goals without going broke in the process. The truth is that in order to achieve most of your goals, you will need some help, no matter what your goals are. Having the right professional help in a divorce will make all the difference in the world in terms of the outcome. This is especially true with regards to the financial outcome.

This book focuses on one of the key tips for winning a divorce financially: **assembling a winning divorce team**.

Because of all the issues involved, Divorces today are usually handled by more than one or two professionals. There are financial issues such as alimony and child support, how to value and divide assets, and how to handle taxes before, during, and after the divorce. Also, if one of the spouses has worked for a corporation, the federal government, or the state, a qualified retirement planning specialist will have to be brought in. Where children are involved, you will have issues around custody, visitation, and parenting plans, which may require the services of a child evaluation specialist. Plus, you may need a child psychologist or therapist to help the child in question deal with any psychological issues as a result of the parents' divorce. Is infidelity an issue? If so, your case may require that an investigator be brought onto the team.

Hopefully, you see the point here: because of complexities and the amount of issues to consider in divorces today, you will need to put together and finance a winning team of professionals. This includes **Finding and Hiring a Winning Divorce Attorney.** Your attorney will be a key team member in your divorce, if not the most important individual on the team. Another key member on your team is a relatively new type of professional, the divorce consultant/advisor. This person works with your attorney on strategy and provides resources to help you win your divorce. There is a whole chapter on the importance of assembling the right team, especially your divorce attorney and divorce consultant, in my soon-to-be-released book, *100 Plus Divorce Tips™: A Guide to Financially Winning Your Divorce.* Go to bookpreview (www.100plusdivorcetips.com/bookpreview) for more information about the book.

I wrote *100 Plus Divorce Tips™: A Guide to Financially Winning Your Divorce* in order to share the many strategies that I learned from research and my experiences with divorce. I share my personal story about how I came out of the divorce process winning big financially.

For me, winning big meant not having to pay any alimony in either case, retaining a jointly-owned New York City condo in my first divorce, gaining full custody of my daughter (it is very rare for men to accomplish this in any U.S. states), and getting to keep several assets that were jointly-owned assets in both of my divorces. This also included retaining business interests that I had. Thinking back, I definitely owe my wins to being strategic in how I handled my divorce cases. My strategy included assembling a great team of talented and experienced divorce professionals to help me win. Looking back, I will admit that my divorces were not easy to win, nor were they inexpensive. But, in the end, I accomplished my primary goal of "financially winning" and coming out ahead on a long-term basis. In my opinion, this result was well worth the time and money that I spent to get it.

I also have experience as a financial advisor to several of the wealthiest families here in the United States. I watched as some of these families battled over millions of dollars. Several also had bitter fights over the custody of their children. Watching the battles was actually very helpful and provided me with some ideas and divorce strategies that are shared in the book.

The research for the book also included conversations with lawyers, certified public accountants, and others who helped me formulate a lot of the tips for winning a divorce. Most importantly, the folks that I spoke with convinced me that one of the key things that people should do to ensure that they have a chance of winning their divorce is to put together the right team and work with that team to plan a strategy for a successful outcome. It is very important to realize that you don't want to go out and hire any old lawyer to handle your divorce case – you need to make sure that you get someone who is competent, and who is an expert on divorce and family law matters in your area.

Ultimately, if you are hoping to win a divorce today, you will need to strategize and plan to win your case. Unfortunately, because of the complexities of our current divorce system, winning will take more than simply hiring a great lawyer. You will actually need to assemble a whole winning team of professionals and specialists to help

4. The 17 Characteristics of a Winning Divorce Attorney

There are thousands of divorce attorneys out there with all kinds of credentials and experience. Here are several of the important characteristics that a winning divorce attorney will have. The questions that are provided in chapters 9, 10, and 11 will help you ascertain if the attorney you are thinking about hiring possesses many of these characteristics.

There are two things to keep in mind with regards to this list. First, when you interview your potential divorce attorney (using the questions), pay attention not only to the attorney's answers to the questions, but also to how the attorney answers you. This will give you clues as to whether they have the characteristics listed below. The tone in their voice, their body language, pausing before they answer the question, etc. all will be great clues.

Second, a winning divorce attorney does not necessarily need to possess all seventeen characteristics. However, in my opinion, there are fourteen key characteristics that you want your attorney to have to increase the odds of winning your divorce.

Here are all seventeen important characteristics. I have placed an asterisk* by the first fourteen key characteristics.

1) *The best divorce attorneys are board-certified and specialize in family law. At least 75 percent of their practices are focused on family law and divorce.

2) *Winning divorce attorneys are great communicators, both orally and in writing. An important part of their jobs is to be able to explain difficult or complex legal concepts and issues and make them easy for you to understand.

3) *The best divorce attorneys are good listeners. They need to be able to *hear* your side of the story, understand you, and be patient with you. They also need to be able to listen to the judge, your spouse's counsel, and any witnesses in your case. Having good listening skills will enable your attorney to better understand what issues are really important to you in your divorce case and therefore enable them to better negotiate and get you exactly what you want. Having a divorce attorney who is a good listener will save you time and money – he or she will get "it" right the first time and fully understand the issues in your case.

4) *A great divorce attorney is aggressive when he or she needs to be, and knows when it is appropriate to be aggressive.

5) *Winning divorce attorneys possess excellent negotiation skills. And, as the saying goes, they know when to hold them and when to fold them.

6) *Great divorce attorneys need to be great at trying cases, in the event that your divorce case ends up being one of the ten percent that actually goes to trial.

7) *Winning divorce attorneys put the client's needs ahead of their own needs, especially when it comes to dealing with children and custody issues.

8) *A winning divorce attorney is trustworthy, honest, and has integrity. He always gives clients his or her best advice and is a straight shooter when it comes to discussing difficult topics with clients. In other words, these attorneys don't sugarcoat information. To win your divorce, you should stick to the facts of your case. The best divorce attorneys are open and honest and should give you the facts so that you can make good decisions. Additionally, trustworthiness is a very important trait for a divorce attorney to possess, given that you will be sharing very intimate details about your life and your desires with your attorney. It's important that you feel comfortable confiding in your divorce attorney.

9) *When there is a lot of money at stake or other business issues, winning divorce attorneys will have some level of competence with numbers, finance, investments, business concepts, economics, and taxes. While they don't have to be full-blown experts in these areas, they should have experience and more than a basic understanding of the concepts so they can give you

advice on these subjects. They should also know when to bring in additional experts.

10)*Winning divorce attorneys have massive rolodexes and access to resources and experts that they might need to help you win your divorce case.

11)*Winning divorce attorneys are hardworking individuals and are reasonably available to their clients during non-business hours. In many divorce cases, clients will need help or advice at some odd time. An example would be how to handle a situation where an abusive spouse shows up at your doorstep at 1:00 AM drunk and bangs on your door, wanting to kiss the kids good night. You want to know what to do? A winning divorce attorney will also properly train clients so that they do not abuse the divorce attorney's availability, and so that the client knows when they might need to call the police.

12)*Winning divorce attorneys are respected by their peers and by the court.

13)*Winning divorce attorneys possess creativity and craftiness. Often, the negotiations in a divorce can be very difficult and it's helpful to have an attorney who can think outside of the box and come up with creative solutions to help you settle your case.

14)*Winning divorce attorneys have winning attitudes. They win most of their cases and have clients that are happy with the results where settlements are involved. You want to hire a divorce attorney who wins most of their cases.

15) The best divorce attorneys need to be compassionate and empathetic individuals. This is a very important trait for divorce attorneys to have, given the amount of emotions involved in all divorce cases.

16) A winning divorce attorney needs to be someone who is confident but not arrogant. Usually, the only person in a divorce case who can get away with being arrogant is the judge.

17) The great divorce attorney has an understanding of human relationships. He or she knows that psychology is important because of the high degree of emotions that one deals with in a divorce.

5. The Divorce Industry – It's a Big Business: Why You Need the Right Attorney to Win Your Divorce

The business of divorce is a multibillion-dollar business here in the United States. I have seen figures that suggest that the industry generates upwards of 100 billion dollars annually. It has become almost common knowledge that approximately fifty percent of all first time marriages that begin out of love and commitment end bitterly in divorce after just a few years. That divorce rate is significantly higher for persons on their second and third marriages.

The fact that the U.S. marriage turnover rate is so high, and that there is so much money involved, means that the divorce and family law industry has attracted many players hoping to stake a financial claim for themselves, regardless of their level of competency or experience in the field. There are many, many hands greedily vying for a piece of the divorce industry pie. This is why you need to be careful. There is a lot at stake in a divorce and the end results are long lasting, so you need to select the right attorney.

There are many attorneys out there to choose from, so finding and hiring the best divorce attorney to be part of your team will take some work. Not all divorce attorneys are equal in their abilities or years of experience, nor will you be compatible with every lawyer that you meet.

So, how exactly do you find and hire the best divorce attorney in your area? While going through my own divorces, I made a bunch of what I will call "rookie" mistakes. These mistakes cost me time and money and caused me a lot of unnecessary stress. This leads me to highlight the point of this book, as well as the reason for my forthcoming book: in going through my divorces and spending time helping other folks with their divorces, I figured out several winning strategies and ways that you can get some of the same results as me.

By implementing some of my tips, you will be able to save a lot of time and money. In addition to my personal experiences, I spent three and a half years researching and reading everything that I could find on the topic. While I was in the financial services industry, I provided investment and financial planning advice, which included providing strategies for individuals going through divorces. My work included helping clients find and secure whatever resources they needed for their divorces, which often included helping them to find divorce attorneys.

6. Tips and Resources for Where to Find a Winning Divorce Attorney

It is very important that you use an attorney who is experienced in family law and handling divorces, and who is, most importantly, compatible with you. According to the American Bar Association, there are over one million attorneys practicing a variety of different types of law in the United States today. However, there are only about ten thousand members of the American Academy of Matrimonial Lawyers (AAML), which is the main association that top family law practitioners belong to in the U.S. I will share more about the AAML later on in this book.

The point that I want to bring to your attention is that only about one percent of all the attorneys out there specialize in handling divorce work. While I am sure that most of all the other 990,000 attorneys are quite competent, well-trained, and skilled at their respective crafts, divorce law is highly specialized. What this means is that if you hire someone to represent you in a divorce who is not a specialist, the chances are that if your spouse does hire a divorce specialist, this will probably greatly reduce your chances of winning your divorce.

To emphasize my point, consider this question: if you needed heart surgery tomorrow to save your life, would you hire your eye doctor to perform the surgery, or would you try to hire the best cardiac surgeon that you could find? The key advice here is: don't bring a knife to a gunfight. Hire the best divorce attorney that you can find and afford.

There are many ways to find a reliable lawyer. I will highlight the **three most effective resources** at your disposal:

- **Friends, family, and other connections**

- **State bar associations**

- **The American Academy of Matrimonial Lawyers (AAML)**

One of the best ways to find a competent divorce attorney is to get a recommendation from a trusted friend or relative, a business associate, another attorney that you might know, or a divorce consultant/advisor. Keep in mind that every legal case is different and that a lawyer who is right for one person may not suit you or your legal problem.

Besides getting attorneys referred from friends and relatives who have had good results, you may also call your local *state bar association* and ask them to give you referrals. Most state bars will give you at least two or three names to select from. One important point about state bar association referrals is that you need to make sure that the association actually has regulatory authority over attorneys in your state. Otherwise, you will not be able to get accurate background information about the attorneys you are checking out. In Virginia, for example, if you Google "Virginia state bar association," you will get two distinct agencies: the "Virginia Bar Association" and the "Virginia State Bar Association." It is the Virginia State Bar Association that disciplines attorneys and would have information on whether an attorney has complaints registered against them.

Each state is different, so make sure you ask the bar association certain questions to get the information that you need. When you call into the state bar association, the first question to ask is, "Are you responsible for disciplining attorneys in your state?" If the answer is yes, you can ask them for a few divorce attorney referrals, but make sure to ask whether the attorney they are referring has any complaints lodged against them. I would recommend avoiding these attorneys.

According to the American Bar Association, eighteen states have programs that certify lawyers as specialists in certain types of law, including family law. These states are Alabama, Arizona, California, Connecticut, Florida, Georgia, Idaho, Indiana, Louisiana, Maine, Minnesota, New Jersey, New Mexico, North Carolina, Pennsylvania, South Carolina, Tennessee, and Texas. To learn more about which types of law are certified in which states, go to www.abanet.org/legal-services/specialization/source.html. In states without certification programs, you may want to ask about your lawyer's areas of specialization.

I mentioned above that there is an association called the American Academy of Matrimonial Lawyers (AAML). In my opinion, the AAML is one of the best resources for finding excellent divorce attorneys in your area. You can reach the AAML at www. aaml.org, or at 312-263-6477. Generally speaking, attorneys that are members of the AAML are some of the most experienced family law practitioners in the country. To be considered for membership in this association, an attorney needs to have family law work represent 75 percent of their total practice. They also need to have at least ten years of experience in family law and must be recognized by the courts and their local bar associations as being experts in the field. The AAML's website lists members by state.

No matter how you find an attorney, check out his or her credentials before you meet. You can get information about the lawyer from the local state bar association and by looking their name up in a directory of lawyers called Martindale-Hubbell, which should be available at your local library or online at www.martindale.com. The Martindale-Hubbell directory is great because besides providing attorney names for your local area, it also provides ratings on individual attorneys and law firms. The site provides two types of ratings and reviews that are based on data that it collects. Firstly, it has a peer review ratings, and secondly, it has a client review section. The information that it provides helps potential clients feel more confident about their decisions to hire attorneys by providing objective indicators of attorney and firm ethics and legal abilities, in addition to highlighting attorney credentials such as college and law schools attended and other important affiliations. The peer reviews provide information on five key areas, including legal knowledge, analytical capabilities, judgment, communication ability, and legal experience. Martindale-Hubbell's "AV Rating" is its highest award for professional ability and ethics.

Two other great resources that you can use to find winning divorce attorneys are the websites www.superlawyers.com and www.lawyer.com. Super Lawyers is an organization and independent rating service of outstanding lawyers from more than seventy different practice areas who have attained a high degree of peer recognition and professional achievement. The selection process is multi-phased and includes independent research, peer nominations, and peer evaluations. *Super Lawyers Magazine* features profiles of selected attorneys and is distributed to attorneys in the state or region and the ABA-accredited law school libraries. Super Lawyers Magazine is also published as a special section in leading city and regional magazines across the country. In the United States, *Super Lawyers Magazine* is published in all fifty states and Washington, D.C., reaching more than thirteen million readers.

WWW.lawyer.com is a lawyer search service that helps users find the best lawyers to suit their needs. The company's database has over 434,000 lawyers in it from all over the United States. The site's advanced search feature allows you to search for attorneys by narrow specializations such as divorce or custody within the more general Family Law area; you can also search for attorneys by gender, find information about whether they are in good standing professionally, find out what year they were admitted to practice, etc. The website is a great tool to use in conjunction with the other sites. It is generally positive if an attorney is listed in more than one of the databases.

Lastly, make sure to check out the personal websites of any attorneys that you are considering hiring. The websites will have a lot of information about them and their law practices.

7.

Does the Gender of Your Divorce Attorney Matter?

The gender of your attorney shouldn't make a difference in whether or not you win your case, but it does. The reasons for this are complicated and have to do with how you are perceived in the courtroom.

Every human has different opinions, experiences, and ways of processing information. This is true for judges as much as it is for anyone else. Judges also tend to have very large egos. I will never forget an experience that I had as a teenager. I got to sit on the bench with a friend of the family, who was a criminal court judge, as part of my high school senior project. The project was to do a report on the legal system and at the same time try to figure out if I thought that I might want to go to law school one day. As part of my project, I was able to sit on the bench with the judge and listen to his arraignments, trials, and hearings over a period of two months. I had private discussions with the judge, who would explain his thought processes and feelings about each case.

It was quite an experience for a teenager. I keenly remember the judge staring at the various attorneys and defendants and quickly formulating his opinions about the individuals just from looking at them, before reading any case papers or hearing the arguments on the matter. Sometimes he would turn to me and make comments like, "This one looks bad,

Chris, I can tell." It was interesting to me that the judge almost never swayed from his initial opinion about the people or case that he was being asked to judge.

The point of me mentioning this story is that I firmly believe that we all do this sizing up. We all make initial judgments about other people based on our first impressions, whether we admit it or not. In the judicial system and in divorce court especially, judges do this all the time.

Keeping this in mind, it is important to note that how you appear before the court and the attorney you pick to represent you will play a large role in determining the outcome of your divorce case. What I mean by how you appear to the court is how the court views you and your entire case as a package. Who your attorney is, whether he or she is a known quality within the jurisdiction in your area, and whether or not he is a respected divorce attorney is important. If, for example, he is a member of the AAML, it means that he has at least 10 years of divorce court experience. If the judge has also been around for a while, there is a high likelihood that the judge knows your attorney and, even better, respects and trusts your attorney. Having an attorney who is known within the professional divorce community is a very important consideration that will make a difference as you plan and strategize your divorce.

Make sure that you select an attorney whom you trust and can connect with, and most importantly, with whom you feel comfortable working. I can't emphasize enough how important it is that you have good chemistry with your divorce attorney. This will be particularly important to you from an emotional standpoint. Feeling comfortable with your attorney will help you with being able to confide in him or her as you work together on strategy to win your case. Also, there is a part of winning your divorce that is psychological and emotional. Being able to fully trust the professionals you work with will help alleviate a lot of the stress generally associated with divorce.

This brings us back to the issue of gender. Besides being compatible with your divorce attorney, you should also look to hire an attorney who complements your personality. For instance, if you are a relatively introverted and quiet woman who has been in a long relationship where your spouse managed all of the financial affairs for the family, my suggestion for you would be to consider hiring a male attorney with a strong, aggressive personality to balance you out. The same thoughts should be taken into consideration if you are a male. If your personality as a male is that of the dominant spouse who handles all of the family's financial affairs and controls most of the family's decisions, look to hire a sharp but very feminine woman attorney who might help to soften up your image. The strategy of whether to hire a male or female attorney might be especially important in a child custody battle.

It is great to go out and hire the best divorce attorney that you can afford. But it is also very important that you find the right strategic fit for your case, which may mean taking gender into account. Incidentally, selecting an attorney who can help with softening up your image does not mean that the attorney should be soft. On the contrary, to win your divorce, you want to hire a ferocious fighter. Your attorney and your divorce consultant will be the two most important members of your divorce team in terms of winning, so it is important that you take the time to find and hire the very best professionals that you can afford and with whom you feel comfortable working.

8. What Type of Law Firm is Best to Win a Divorce?

There are many different types of law firms out there: everything from large multinational law firms to medium and small-sized boutique law firms and even solo practitioner firms.

Because family law is so specialized, my personal preference is to hire a divorce attorney who is part of a smaller firm or medium firm that specializes in this area of the law and has adequate support staff. I think that there are some advantages in working with a firm like this in terms of them being able to produce high-quality work efficiently and in a timely manner. Also, many smaller firms that specialize in divorce generally have great internal resources available to help tackle even the most difficult problems that might arise in a case. They won't have to scramble and waste time looking for outside resources if some issue comes up in your divorce where they need to bring in an expert, such as a forensic accountant to find missing assets. The firm would already have a stable of these types of resources available that they use regularly to help win their cases.

Another benefit of some of the smaller divorce firms is that the reputation of the firm and its lawyers can intimidate opponents into settling quickly, or at least help to keep your spouse's attorney reasonable in your settlement negotiations. Your goal should be to come to terms and settle quickly with your spouse in order to avoid the legal fees of a long, drawn-out case. Some smaller divorce firms also have in-house certified public accountants, financial planners, and even investigators on staff, which can help to keep the total costs of your divorce down.

In my second divorce case, the attorney that I initially hired was a sole practitioner. She had just one paralegal, and unfortunately for me, she had several cases that she was juggling at the same time. When I called her office, I would often get an answering service or sometimes her answering machine. When I had important questions, it would sometimes take two or three days for the attorney to return my phone calls, and the same was true for emails that I sent her. Not hearing back from my attorney for two or three days was extremely frustrating to me, which caused both my anxiety level and my blood pressure to rise significantly. The behavior was unacceptable and I really allowed the neglect to go on for longer than I should have before confronting the attorney with the situation.

I made a big mistake in working with an attorney who took her sweet time getting back to me. I never had a discussion with the attorney up front about how and when we would communicate with each other, so I never fully got comfortable with working with her. Eventually, I ended up firing her and replacing her with an attorney at a great small firm that had lots of resources and the killer, intimidating reputation that I refer to above.

In a nutshell, don't make the mistake of hiring a sole practitioner who is unable to give you the level of communication that you need. It is also critical that you ask any potential attorney about the depth of their organization and their support staff up front. You should only hire an attorney that has adequate resources and support staff to handle the total number of cases that they have at any given time. You definitely do not want to hire an attorney who is stretched too thin and will not be able to give your case the amount of focused attention that you need in order to win. This point leads me to the next set of tips that I have for you, which center around what questions you should be asking of yourself and of any divorce attorney.

9. Important Questions to Ask Yourself Before Hiring a Divorce Attorney

☞ **"Who greeted me when I entered the attorney's office?"**

☝ In my opinion, first impressions are very important. They will help you figure out whether you are going to be compatible with the attorney. If the attorney greets you himself, it could mean that he really cares about his clients. He or she is glad to see you and wants you to feel at ease and welcome. It might mean that he is not rigid or cold.

☞ **"Do I feel comfortable in the attorney's reception area? Was I offered a beverage?"**

☝ To me, this shows a courteous and thoughtful professional. Again, the attorney wants you to feel like a welcomed guest. It's not the end of the world if they don't offer you a beverage, but I believe small gestures like this show that the attorney cares, pays attention to small details, and acts professional. Also, they want you to relax as much as possible before your meeting.

☞ **"What does the inside of the attorney's office look like? Does the office appear neat and organized? Are there expensive paintings on the walls? Does he or she have pictures of their**

family displayed? Are there law books in the bookcases?"

☝ A disorganized office could mean a disorganized mind or a sloppy professional. This is something you want to pay attention to. Expensive artwork suggests success and pride in the office.

☞ **"How long does the attorney have me wait before he sees me?"**

☝ This could provide a hint about the attorney's ability to manage time efficiently, but it could also simply mean that they were on an important call with another client.

☞ **"Is the office quiet and calm, or does it seem frantic?"**

☞ **"Is the office convenient for me to get to from my home and office?"**

☞ **"Do I get the impression that the attorney is successful?"**

☞ **"Does the attorney take calls while he is speaking with me?"**

☞ **"How is the attorney dressed? Does he look like a winner to me?"**

☝ Presentation and attention to detail are extremely important.

10. Deal-breakers: Four "Must-Haves" for Your Divorce Attorney Shortlist

1) **Is the attorney board-certified in family law in your state?**

   If not, you probably don't need to waste valuable time setting up a meeting with this person. Board certification speaks to the important winning characteristics of experience, professionalism, dedication, knowledge, and expertise in the field. You want to stack the odds of winning your divorce in your favor, so I recommend that you stick with attorneys who specialize in family law and are up to speed on any current issues in the field. You can usually find out if an attorney is board-certified in family law from the state's bar association. If the attorney has a website, it will probably mention this fact there as well.

2) **Does the attorney you are considering have expertise in a particular sub-category of family law that you need?**

   Examples of some sub-categories where additional expertise might be required are child custody, same-sex marriage and divorce, military divorce, and more. To win a divorce case that involves issues with any of these sub-categories, you need an attorney who is very familiar with these special areas of the law. In the case of a same-sex couple going through a breakup and divorce, there is a great deal of complexity, uncertainty and ambiguity in these cases due to the novelty of this legal area. As of the writing of this book (May 2014), same-sex marriage is only recognized in 17 states and the District of Columbia. If a non-traditional couple gets married in a state where same-sex marriage is recognized, then moves to a state where same-sex marriage is not recognized and wants to get a divorce, the divorce in the new state is nearly impossible to obtain, let alone settle in a financially equitable way. In addition, in October 2013, the Supreme Court made a ruling that in terms of federal law, same-sex couples are now entitled to the same federal benefits that other couples receive as long as the same-sex couple is legally married. The point here is that you need an attorney who is an expert in this area to give you the right advice if you are going to win your divorce. Incidentally, the 17 states that have legalized same-sex marriage are California, Connecticut, Delaware, Hawaii, Illinois, Iowa, Maine, Maryland, Massachusetts, Minnesota, New Hampshire, New Jersey, New Mexico, New York, Rhode Island, Vermont, and Washington. The District of Columbia is also included in this group. Other states will follow suit as time goes on, which will hopefully help to make it easier for same-sex couples to divorce in the future.

3) Does the divorce attorney have any complaints against them?

How to obtain this information is discussed in chapter 6. Basically, avoid attorneys who have legitimate client complaints against them. You may want to speak with the attorney directly about a complaint should all of the other shortlist questions be answered favorably. Because of the high level of emotions involved in divorces, it is possible that a client might file a bogus complaint against an attorney. When I was in the securities industry, this happened quite often. Make sure that if there is a complaint, you find out the result of the complaint and whether there was any sanction or punishment imposed.

4) Is the divorce attorney affordable to you?

In earlier chapters of this book, I talk about the costs involved in hiring a winning divorce attorney. Divorce is expensive! The best divorce attorneys that get the best results consistently are not cheap. My advice is that you stretch as much as you can afford to in terms of which attorney you hire, and then follow the tips on divorce cost management that are in my soon-to-be-released book, *100 Plus Tips™: A Guide to Financially Winning Your Divorce.*

11. Important Questions to Ask Your Divorce Attorney

Note: some of the answers to these questions can be obtained from the local state bar association in advance of your meeting.

☞ **"Where did you go to law school and what year did you graduate?"**

☞ **"How long have you been practicing this type of law?"**

👍 My suggestion is that you want someone with seven to ten years of experience, unless the person works at a law firm where they have a mentor and access to more experienced attorneys for consulting. If you do end up with a more junior attorney, you should ask this follow-up question:

☞ **"How will I be charged in the event that you [the junior attorney] need to consult one of the senior attorneys?"**

👍 You do not want to have to pay for your junior attorney's tuition, nor do you want to be billed for two attorneys' hourly fees. You might agree that in such cases where a more experienced attorney is giving guidance to his/her junior associate, you would only pay one fee, which would be at the hourly rate of the more experienced attorney. Better still, you might agree on a blended hourly rate that is higher than the junior associate's rate but lower than that of the senior attorney. Whatever you ultimately agree upon, these discussions should be had in advance. I think that this is a very fair way to handle these types of situations.

☞ **"How many divorce cases have you handled in the past six months? What were the outcomes of the cases? How many cases are you currently handling?"**

👍 You want to make sure that you are getting an experienced divorce attorney. You also want to make sure that your attorney is not too busy to give your case the attention it deserves. Keep in mind that if an attorney has only had a few cases over a six-month period of time, it could mean that they simply had some large and complicated cases. The key for you is making sure that the attorney you are considering will have time to devote to your case and that the amount of time is enough to win your divorce.

☞ **"How do you charge? Do you bill on the ¼ hour or ½ hour [every fifteen or thirty minutes]?"**

👍 It is best to discuss billing and hourly rates up front.

☞ **"Are they pass-through charges, or do you mark up the expenses?"**

☝ Find out what your attorney charges for expenses, such as coping documents and messengers.

☞ **"Will I need to provide a retainer?"**

☝ A retainer is basically a down payment on your attorney's future services. This is common practice and should be expected. It is usually a few thousand dollars. In some very complex cases where there are a lot of assets involved, I have seen retainers as high as $25,000 or even $50,000. Attorneys generally have a standard retainer amount that they require in order to take you on as a client and get your case started. They will work off of this balance, which will be held in an account for you. If the amount becomes depleted, he or she will ask you for another deposit. Also, you will get monthly statements that will show exactly where your money is being spent and how much of your retainer is left.

☞ **"Can you estimate the total cost of my case?"**

☝ While it will be difficult to know the exact number, an experienced attorney should be able to ballpark the cost. Do not be surprised to hear a number that is well above $20,000 or even a lot more, depending on the case and the amount of assets involved. Payments can often be worked out with the attorney afterwards; however, I would suggest that you work out the details and payment schedule in advance.

Attorneys need to be paid and you should keep in mind when discussing fees that you want the attorney to feel good about working with you. You also want to make sure that you do not give them the impression that it will be difficult to collect their payments from you. You need to make them feel that you will pay your legal bills promptly.

☞ **"Is my method of payment okay?"**

👍 You should discuss your method of payment with the attorney in advance. Let him know whether you will be paying in cash, by check, or with a credit card. In the *100 Plus Divorce Tips*™ book, I provide a lot of tips on how to keep your divorce costs down.

I also talk about a new method of financing your divorce should you be strapped for cash while you are working on a settlement. There are a few investment firms that specialize in financing divorces in exchange for an agreed-upon return on the money that they lend you. While this is a new trend in the divorce arena, it makes a lot of sense to explore this type of option in cases where one spouse controls a family's assets and as a result can hire the best attorneys to try and take advantage of the other spouse.

If you would like to know more about financing the costs of your divorce, feel free to send me an email at chris@100plusdivorcetips.com.

☞ **"Who will be working on my case?"**

👍 If you meet with a top partner at the law firm, ask or clarify that the top partner attorney will in fact be working on your case and that he or she will not simply be pawning your case off to a junior attorney. You want to make sure that you get what you are paying for. If he is handing off your case, what will be the extent of his involvement?

☞ **"What other specialists will you need to bring in?"**

👍 Specialists can include divorce coaches/advisors, financial planners, forensic accountants, qualified retirement plan specialists, child evaluation specialists, and so on. Any of these could be important team members in helping you to win your divorce. All of these additional specialists will have to be paid, and their costs could be substantial. Again, I want to refer you to my other book, which has lots of suggestions for ways to help reduce and manage the costs of a divorce.

☞ **"How long do you estimate the case will take from start to finish?"**

👍 The answer to this will vary depending on the complexity of the case. The time it takes to complete your divorce will also be affected by the busyness of the court's calendar.

12. Win Your Divorce: Stack the Odds in Your Favor

One last very important tip that I want to give you about hiring a divorce attorney is to always remember two basic rules:

1. **There are no free lunches in the divorce business**

2. **Do not hire a divorce attorney just because they give you the lowest price**

Pay or invest a bit more into the expense of your divorce so you can stack the odds in your favor. Remember, the decisions you make will affect you for a long, long time.

To conclude, in order to financially win your divorce case, it is very important that you hire the **best attorney for you**. Attorneys are critical to winning, so it is important that you get along with your attorney and that he or she is experienced in family law. The attorney that you hire should be an experienced tiger who gives your case the time and resources it deserves. The bottom line is that your attorney can make a huge difference in determining the outcome of your divorce, so you must choose wisely. Good luck!

About the Author:

Chris Dunnaville spent thirty years on Wall Street at Morgan Stanley Smith Barney and US Trust as a financial advisor and private banker to some of the wealthiest families in the United States. Today, he resides in Portland, Oregon with his fourteen-year-old daughter and their chocolate Lab. He is an entrepreneur, philanthropist, college professor, and divorce consultant, and the author of the soon-to-be-released book, *100 Plus Divorce Tips™: A Guide to Financially Winning Your Divorce*. For more information on the book go to www.100plusdivorcetips.com/bookpreview Professor Dunnaville conducts seminars and workshops on various financial topics.

To inquire about Professor Dunnaville's Divorce Coaching and Advisory Services, feel free to email him at the following address: chris@100plusdivorcetips.com.

Notes

_____

_____

_____

_____

_____

_____

_____

_____

_____

_____

_____

_____

_____

_____

_____

_____

_____

_____

_____

_____

_____

_____

_____

_____

_____

_____

Notes

_____

_____

_____

_____

_____

_____

_____

_____

_____

_____

_____

_____

_____

_____

_____

_____

_____

_____

_____

_____

_____

_____

_____

_____

_____

_____

_____

_____

Notes

www.ingramcontent.com/pod-product-compliance
Lightning Source LLC
Chambersburg PA
CBHW061756040426
42447CB00011B/2321